The Image
of
CHRIST

Rolando Z. Garcia

ISBN 979-8-88943-852-6 (paperback)
ISBN 979-8-88943-853-3 (digital)

Christian Faith Publishing
832 Park Avenue
Meadville, PA 16335
www.christianfaithpublishing.com

Printed in the United States of America

CHAPTER 1

Finding the Jews in a Cave

Farmer Ishamel came from the village of Eilat where he lived with his wife and son. A modest family that farmed goats and sheep for a living. His wife, Esther, took care of some chickens and the household. The son, Abram, seventeen years old, was bright for his age and always looking for ways to raise income for the family. He attended the village school and helped his family on the farm.

Workdays started early for the family. Animals had to be fed and cared for. As always, Esther's chickens produced enough eggs for breakfast. Warm homemade bread, eggs, and goat milk were served, and Ishamel enjoyed his coffee and tea.

"Come, Abram, eat, for we have to take the sheep and goats down to the pasture before the morning gets hot," the family gathered with a prayer at the table, and Esther, as always, shared a joke to cheer up the family.

Young Abram, as always, thought about life outside his village walls. His studies drew him to books and what life in the city was like.

Two local shepherds with their goats and sheep were always looking for anything of value to supplement their income while also guarding the few goats and sheep in the area.

Ishamel and his son took the dozen or so goats and sheep into the pasture below the hills, close to the village about a mile and a half away. Ishamel had always gone to this area; the grass was good year-round, and there were a couple of water ponds from the rains that came down from the hills. The hills were covered with broken pieces of cracked rock.

"Abram, look up toward the peak. It looks like a cave or hole in the cliff has opened up," Ishamel said.

"Father, should I go up and see if it's a cave? I'll be careful for snakes or creepy creatures and falling rocks," Abram responded.

Abram slowly climbed to the crevice and made sure nothing was inside the opening of the rock.

"Be careful, son. Something might be in there," Ishamel called out.

Abram continued to throw rocks into the hole.

"Father, it looks empty. Bring me the oil lamp so we can look inside," Abram said.

"It looks like there are three big sealed jars," Ishamel observed.

"Be careful for falling rocks. Can you pull them out very carefully?" Ishamel asked.

"Yes, they are a little heavy," Abram replied.

"Be careful and don't drop them. Wait, I'll help you carry them down," Ishamel offered.

Abram and Ishamel managed to bring the jars down and were amazed by the find, hoping to discover gold or jewels. "Ishamel, I'm going down to the house to bring our donkey to carry them out. Abram, don't tell anybody about the jars," Ishamel instructed. While waiting, Abram pondered what could be inside and hoped for gold or jewelry.

Ishamel returned with the donkey and secured the three jars to it, covering them with cut grass to hide them from the villagers. They slowly made their way down the canyon with the loaded donkey, eventually hiding the jars inside the small barn where the sheep and goats were kept.

As Ishamel covered the jars, Abram dreamt of the jewels or gold they might sell for a profit, allowing them to acquire more goats, sheep, oil for the home, and something special for the family.

"Dad, let's open the jars and see what's inside," Abram eagerly suggested.

"Patience, my son. Everything will fall into place. Let's inform the family and eat first. We need to tend to the goats and sheep, give them water and feed," Ishamel replied.

When they arrived home, Esther, Abram's wife, inquired about the items on the donkey. "It looks like rocks. What are they?" she asked.

"No, my wife, they are jars we found in a cave near the hills. We haven't opened them yet. They were covered in that cave for a long time. Perhaps they contain scrolls like the ones found years ago that could bring a small fortune and supplement our income. Only God knows what's inside. We'll open them the next day. For now, let's eat and thank God for our simple life and the possibilities ahead," Ishamel explained.

Son Abram pondered during their meal about what could be inside the jars. *I hope it's gold or something valuable. It would help with my studies and the family*, he thought. After dinner, young Abram took care of the goats and sheep, feeding them and settling them for the night. As he got ready for bed, it was difficult for him to fall asleep. Meanwhile, his dad soundly slept, snoring loudly throughout the night.

CHAPTER 2

The Journey

The sun couldn't come soon enough for young Abram. *What's in those jars?* he wondered while his dad slowly emerged from his cot.

"God, what a cold morning. Hot tea, woman!" exclaimed Ishamel. "Son, Abram, hurry up, get up and eat so we can open the jars and hope to find something good. Oh, woman, God is good today."

After breakfast, the two walked up to the barn, and Ishamel told young Abram to feed the goats and sheep and make sure they had water.

Young Abram couldn't wait to open those jars. Ishamel called out, "Abram, come here and help me pick them up, and let's find out what's inside those jars."

Ishamel said a little prayer, "Bring us luck and fortune for my family, O Lord."

Ishamel instructed Abram to bring one of the jars to the patio table. Abram hugged the jar tightly and laid it down in front of his father. Ishamel began to blow away the dust on top, noticing how well it was sealed and realizing its age. He used his knife to cut through the cloth and clay that sealed it. Ishamel carefully removed the cloth and looked inside. He saw some kind of scrolls, dusty and old. He took them out of the first jar and laid them on the table with great care. Abram noticed there were five rolls, and he immediately recognized them as scrolls similar to the ones found in the Dead Sea caves. As he unrolled one scroll, he saw ancient writing that hadn't been used in years.

Ishamel left the other scroll inside and told young Abram to bring the second jar. Abram hugged the jar and laid it beside his father. He started to cut the cloth off it, and as he peeled the cloth off, a swift breeze hit his face from inside the jar. Ishamel stood back, staring at his son as they exchanged glances. Ishamel looked inside again and saw more scrolls at the bottom, but he also noticed something shining—an object that appeared to be made of gold and adorned with beautiful colored stones.

"Abram."

"What is it, Father?" Abram asked.

Ishamel smiled and looked at his son, his hands shaking as he pulled out the scrolls from the bottom of the second jar and placed them on the table. He noticed that these scrolls were wrapped with more care and sealed more securely than the others. One of them was even wrapped with ribbons. Slowly, Ishamel cut the ribbon and unwrapped the scroll little by little, being careful not to tear or damage it, as it was extremely old.

Slowly, slowly, Ishamel laid out the scroll on the table and rolled it flat, unraveling it bit by bit. Young Abram's eyes widened with anticipation, eager to see what was inside this ancient scroll. As the scroll unfurled, a painting started to emerge, gradually revealing a face. A strange sensation came over both of them, accompanied by a sweet breeze carrying a hint of unfamiliar fragrance. It was the first time they had ever seen a drawing of someone from thousands of years ago. Young Abram couldn't shake the feeling that he had seen this face before or that it resembled someone he knew.

After finally laying out the entire scroll on the table, Ishamel recoiled in shock when he saw a name, *Yahweh*, written in a Hebrew language that hadn't been spoken in centuries. His son looked at him, noticing his father's pale face. "Father, what is it? Father, what is it?" young Abram asked, concerned. He observed his father's expression, as if he had seen a ghost, with Ishamel's eyes wide and filled with astonishment.

"What, Dad? What did you see?" young Abram asked eagerly.

His father replied, "Son, we have a drawing or painting of Yahweh, Jesus's face. It's a miracle that someone drew him centuries ago. Do you know what this means?" Young Abram remained silent, absorbing the significance of the discovery. His father continued, "This could be worth a lot of money in the hands of the right collector. We have to be careful about who we tell and keep the gold and stones a secret, even from your mother, until we find someone we can trust."

Ishamel looked at his son, holding his hand, and started to dance in excitement. Young Abram began to grasp the gravity of the situation and joined his father in the dance. "We have to be careful about how we handle this. We need to hide the jars and securely store the scroll," Ishamel explained. "We'll take the other scroll to someone important in the city and see what we can get. But we mustn't reveal the drawing until we find someone we can trust and ensure we benefit from this. It's important that the right people see it. This find is of historical significance. We'll sell the gold in the city and open an account in the country bank to keep it safe for the family."

"This is history—a drawing of Jesus and what he really looked like thousands of years ago. Who drew him, and how did it end up buried here in the hills? Come, son, help me store the jars in a safe hiding place, and remember, tell no one," Ishamel instructed.

Ishamel and young Abram entered the house. "Well, Esther," Ishamel began, "what do you think we found in those jars? Come on, guess!" He looked at his son and started dancing around Esther. "Join us and be happy!"

Esther looked at both of them with a puzzled expression. "Are you both crazy? What's going on?"

Ishamel and his son laughed and pulled Esther into the dance. "Dance, woman, for we are going to be rich! Praise God! Praise God! Esther, we've found something amazing!"

Young Abram took his mother's hand and placed a gold chain and two beautiful stones in it. Esther's eyes widened with surprise, and she smiled, joining in the celebration. As the family rejoiced, the scrolls were carefully hidden in the goats' and sheep's hut. The drawing of Yahweh emitted its own soft glow, warming the animals as if conveying peace and joy. The livestock howled in joyous response.

Ishamel heard the commotion and wondered what was happening with the goats and sheep. "I hope that donkey hasn't kicked any of them. That's one mean donkey, but very helpful and strong," he thought. The family continued to dance, pray, and express gratitude for the discovery and the happiness it would bring them.

"Tomorrow, we will begin our journey into the city to find someone who can help us. Now, sleep and remember, tell no one," Ishamel instructed.

Abram tied one jar to the donkey and made sure it was secure. He only put three of the scrolls found in the first jar, intentionally keeping the number a secret from others. The scroll with Jesus's drawing/painting remained hidden back at home.

Abram, come on, let's get started. It's a long walk to the city, and we need to find an honest dealer who can provide us with buyer names and a good price. But finding an honest dealer is not easy.

Abram asked his father, "Father, why don't we ask a teacher or scholar who would know what the scrolls are and what is written on them? Maybe we can get more money for them. And let's not tell anyone about the other scrolls and the drawing of Jesus."

They arrived in the small city and looked around for a place where they would feel comfortable asking questions. Young Abram's eyes were wide with curiosity as he observed the items for sale in the shops and watched young men and women walking around with their phones and fashionable clothes. It was a strange world to him.

They spent hours looking and asking questions to the shopkeepers, trying not to reveal what they had found. Asking about old relics proved to be challenging, as some people eyed them suspiciously, thinking they might be grave robbers.

Looking and asking was not easy. They often received vague or unhelpful answers, and it seemed like no one knew anything about the scrolls. Father and son were growing weary and began to contemplate the long walk back home with nothing to show for their efforts.

"Come on, son, let's eat something before we head back." They sat at a small eating place, discussing how to find someone with knowledge about old relics. As they talked, another young man overheard their conversation. He was a waiter working at the café, and both the son and father looked at him cautiously, unsure of what to say.

The young man asked, "Are you looking for someone who buys old relics? I know of such a person. He is a teacher or professor who specializes in the history of this area. He resides in the next town at the School of Learning."

Abram and his father exchanged glances, contemplating whether they could trust this young man with their find. The young man named Jacob sensed their hesitation and said, "If you don't want to tell me what it is you have to sell, I understand. My name is Jacob. Look, son, we are simple farmers from a small village with limited means. Any money we make will go to support our family. If you can help us, we will compensate you for your time and information."

Jacob replied, "I understand. I come from a small village too. My family are also farmers like yours. My father sent me to the city to study and educate myself for a better living, to help support my family. Whatever little money I earn, I send half of it to them."

Ishamel looked at Abram and smiled, silently expressing gratitude to God. "Praise God, praise," he whispered. Although they hadn't disclosed their discovery to Jacob yet, a little faith and trust had to be established. "Alright, let's eat and find a place to stay for the night," Ishamel suggested.

Jacob quickly interjected, "No, no, you can stay at my place. It's small, but warm and dry." They sat down and engaged in conversation, trying to learn more about Jacob. Young Abram was thrilled to be staying there, fascinated by the small TV and radio. "One day, I will be like Jacob and live in the city," he dreamed.

The following morning, the three of them had a modest breakfast, picked up the donkey with its load, and set off for the next town, where Jacob would introduce them to the teacher. Along the way, young Abram and Jacob talked about the future and their families back on the farm, sharing dreams and exchanging laughter, feeling a sense of closeness between them.

Arriving at the next town, they passed by the school where the teacher worked and studied. The teacher's house was located at the edge of town, not far from the school. As they approached the teacher's house, Ishamel and Jacob exchanged impressed glances. Jacob went to the door and knocked. An older gentleman with a long white beard emerged and smiled. "Ah, Jacob, my lost student! What brings you to visit me? It's been a while since I've seen you. Is there a special occasion? Come in, and who are your friends?"

Jacob introduced Ishamel and Abram to the professor, who introduced himself as Eleazer, a teacher and professor at the local school. "I teach history to the local children," he explained. "What brings you here, my friends? Jacob, it's been a long time, but good to see you, my student. Come on in, and let's have some cookies and tea. Let's talk. You've come from far, and how can I help you?"

"Well, Professor, we found some ancient relics in a cave, stored in jars in the hills near our farm, close to the pasture where we take our goats and sheep," Ishamel began. "We would like for you to assess these items as they are old, and we hope that something like this could be worth some money. We are humble shepherds, and it would greatly help our family and our village. However, we need to trust in your honesty. Once we show you what we've found—"

Eleazer nodded understandingly and reassured them, "I give you my word as a teacher and as a fellow farmer. Farmers like you and me have an honest profession, and we hold respect for the earth we till and the food we grow. Please understand that God has granted me the knowledge to teach our young men and women, just like my friend Jacob."

Ishamel and Abram exchanged smiles and expressed their gratitude to the professor for his kindness and for opening his home to strangers. They asked for his patience as they were new to the city, and they hoped he would accept their honesty in seeking his knowledge in the field of history. They then proceeded to bring the jars into the teacher's house, carefully placing them in a designated spot.

"Here, we've placed them here," Ishamel said as his eyes widened upon seeing the ancient jars. He removed the top cover of one of the jars and reached inside, pulling out the three scrolls. He placed them on a table near the window to benefit from the natural light. The teacher's excitement grew, and his hands trembled as he touched the scrolls and helped them carefully spread them out.

As the scrolls were laid out, the teacher recognized the ancient Hebrew language on the scrolls, a language not spoken for centuries since the time of Jesus. He explained to Ishamel and Abram that the writings on the scrolls detailed Jesus's visit to the village of Babel and his teachings on the word of God. The scrolls were written by an unknown individual from that village, not one of Jesus's apostles.

The professor continued to examine the writings, realizing the significance of the document detailing Jesus's visit and his interactions with his apostles. He informed Ishamel and Jacob that there were individuals who would be highly interested in such a historical artifact and willing to pay a substantial price for it. These important collectors often displayed such relics in museums. However, the authenticity of the document would need to be verified before any transactions could take place.

Ishamel and Jacob expressed their trust in both the professor and Jacob, emphasizing their willingness to share any profits from the sale of the scrolls as a token of gratitude for their time and honesty. They acknowledged the long journey they had undertaken and considered it a divine blessing to have found friends like the professor and Jacob.

Ishamel entrusted the task of making arrangements and negotiating a fair price to himself, indicating that he would inform the professor about the additional scroll they had found in the other two jars. The professor, intrigued, turned to them and inquired about the other jars and scrolls, expressing his curiosity and eagerness to see what they had discovered. Ishamel smiled and replied, confirming that they indeed had two more jars with scrolls, including one that he believed the professor would find particularly fascinating.

"Well, come on down to our village, and we can show you the rest of them, including the most important one that I know you will like, Professor Eleazer," said Ishamel.

Curious, the professor asked what it was about. Ishamel assured him that this particular scroll would both shock and please him.

"You can see for yourself how well-preserved they are, with clear writing and distinct drawings," Ishamel continued. The professor was intrigued, asking about the drawings. Ishamel and his son exchanged smiles while Jacob looked at them with anticipation, sensing that something surprising was about to unfold.

"So, you mean you have more drawings and writings? I can't wait to see them. Come, let's eat something and get some rest. My house is your home," the professor warmly invited.

Abram and young Jacob engaged in lively conversation and laughter while Ishamel and the professor discussed the village and their shared farming backgrounds.

The following morning, the four of them packed their belongings onto the donkey and prepared for the journey back to the village. Excitement filled the air, and Abram and Jacob continued their cheerful banter throughout the trip. Along the way, the professor conversed with Ishamel, discussing the discovery of the cave near the village and how this newfound fortune would benefit his family and the village as a whole. Ishamel expressed his desire for Abram to pursue education outside the village, broadening his horizons and experiencing the world beyond. The professor and Jacob were assured that they would be included in the sharing of the profits as their assistance had been invaluable in preserving the relics. The camaraderie between them resembled that of brothers.

"Abram has only us. He doesn't have any siblings. But, Professor, soon you will see the village and experience the discovery of a lifetime," Ishamel concluded with confidence and gratitude.

As they came to the crest of the road, the village came into view. Ah, it was a splendid morning with the sun just rising, casting a golden glow on the hills. Ishamel couldn't help but think about his much-desired cup of coffee or tea. Hearing Abram's shout, he instructed him to run down to the house and inform his mother that they had company. "Run, Abram, and take Jacob with you. Tell her to heat up some hot coffee and tea," he urged.

Professor Eleazar's eyes widened as he felt a sense of familiarity, reminiscent of his own farm. The open fields and the gleaming pasture resembled a sea in the wind's gentle embrace. The homes where families worked the land in harmony with God's blessings welcomed him back. Ishamel smiled, feeling a deep sense of belonging. *I'm home again*, he thought.

"Mother, Mother, we're home! We have company with us. This is Jacob, and Father is right behind us with the professor," Abram exclaimed.

Esther's smile widened upon seeing her son and, in the distance, her husband. Her eyes filled with joy, knowing her family was safe and back home. Abram ran into her arms, expressing his elation. Esther then returned to the house to warm up some coffee and tea.

Ishamel opened the door with a broad smile as he entered, and Esther rushed to give him a warm hug. "Ah, home! God is good, woman," he exclaimed. Turning to the professor, he introduced him as their friend from the city who would assist them with their discovery. Esther extended a warm welcome, considering their home as the professor's as well.

"Make yourself at home. The professor is from the city of Babel, and they will help us find buyers for the old relics," she explained.

"Sit, professor, and enjoy hot tea and coffee along with a warm breakfast. Tell us about your studies and teaching in the city, as well as where you came from. We are but humble farmers and live our lives according to our Lord's teachings," Ishamel suggested. The professor began discussing both life in the city and on the farm, sharing his experiences.

Ishamel stood up and said, "Come on, let's show you the rest of the relics." The professor's excitement grew as he anticipated seeing them. "And, professor, wait until you see the surprise on your face when I show you the scroll with the drawing," Ishamel added. They all walked to the back of the stable, where Ishamel reached for a board next to a box hidden among the goats and sheep. He pulled away the cover and grass, revealing the spot where the jars were hidden.

The professor and Jacob looked inside and exchanged smiles upon seeing the three jars. Abram and Jacob carefully pulled them out with great excitement, embracing them tightly. Ishamel directed the boys to bring the jars over to the table, placing them near the light, and urged caution as the professor had traveled a long way to see them.

Ishamel extracted the first scroll and laid it on the table for the professor to study. With great care, the professor unrolled the scroll, ensuring it remained undamaged. The expression of joy on the professor's face was evident as he exclaimed, "Oh my God!"

The professor's eyes widened with excitement as he read the scroll detailing the life of a man named Jesus and his apostles, traveling from village to village to teach the word of the Lord. Ishamel called out to the professor, inviting him to take a closer look at something he had found—a combination of writing and drawing.

"By God," said the professor, "it's a description of the village and the daily life of Jesus and his followers." The professor realized it would take months to decipher and translate it into Hebrew, but he was confident that the city's museum would pay a generous price for such a discovery.

Ishamel and his son exchanged smiles, joined by Jacob who shared in their joy. Jacob inquired about whom they could contact and trust to keep the find a secret. The professor replied, "Yes, I know someone in Jerusalem who heads the museum. We must be careful about whom we inform as this is a significant find."

"Ishamel," the professor said, "It's important to hide and be careful not to damage any of the scrolls."

Ishamel replied, "Yes, but are you ready for the best find?"

Eleazar looked at him with curiosity, wondering if there was more to discover. Abram smiled and exchanged glances with Jacob, sharing a moment of laughter.

Ishamel approached the table with another scroll he had retrieved from the jars. This particular scroll was wrapped in cloth and handled delicately, as if cradling a baby. Ishamel placed the bundle on the table and began to gently unravel the cloth, ensuring none of its parts were torn. Professor Eleazar watched with anticipation, eager to see what lay inside. "Come, Professor, help me unroll this scroll," Ishamel invited.

"We must be extremely careful with this one," Ishamel cautioned as both he and the professor started to unroll it.

With each passing turn, a drawing gradually emerged, capturing their attention. The professor's hands trembled, and he wiped the sweat from his face and palms. As the scroll was completely unraveled, his eyes widened with joy. And there it was—the name *Yahweh*, a language used during the time of Jesus.

"My God, Ishamel!" the professor exclaimed.

A rush of sweet air seemed to fill the stable, accompanied by the joyful cries of the animals. The professor, for the first time, witnessed a drawing of Yahweh and what he may have looked like—a depiction by an unknown artist from their very village.

"If we can prove this is not a forgery and that the artist truly lived in this village during Jesus's visit, this is priceless. We must be cautious about who learns of this. Ishamel, this scroll must be securely preserved. You have discovered the eighth wonder of the world. We need to take photographs of everything as a record."

Ishamel called out to Abram and Jacob, instructing them to go to the store and purchase a camera. He provided them with money and emphasized the need for secrecy.

Abram and Jacob were overjoyed and ran off down the road. Ishamel realized the significance of this discovery, not only for his family but for the entire village. "We are all wealthy. Praise God, praise God that we found both of you," he expressed.

"We will need glass jars that can be tightly sealed to prevent any air from entering," the professor explained. "After we take the pictures, we must secure and hide the scrolls in a safe place. If word gets out, there will be individuals trying to deceive or steal from us."

Esther pondered the situation and remarked, "If what you have told me is true, about finding a drawing of Jesus, then the church should know about it."

The professor agreed but cautioned that they needed to proceed with caution. It was a discovery of a lifetime, and many people would oppose the truth.

Esther then mused, "Well, if it means wealth, riches, and our village being known around the world, perhaps I can buy a fine pot and a goat."

Ishamel and the professor laughed in response.

"Oh my God," Esther exclaimed, nearly fainting from the excitement.

"Ishamel, I need to make arrangements to go to Jerusalem and speak with some museum curators. I will take one of the scrolls to show them, but you must hide the rest and not let them know about the other jars. I want to gauge their reaction so we can prove that these are authentic. Then we can discuss prices and security with them as once this information gets out, there will be attempts to steal or make offers.

"Alright, let's set our plan in motion and carefully hide the jars and place the scrolls inside. I have a long day ahead of me tomorrow, so let's get some rest and have more of that tea. Ishamel, sit with me while I go to the museum in Jerusalem and speak with the curators. There is much work to be done, but we must keep it private.

Come, Professor, let's enjoy some hot tea and inform your wife of this incredible discovery. Yes, Ishamel, it is a remarkable find. To have the only drawing of Jesus, showing what he truly looked like, is a blessing. Now the world will truly know the appearance of Jesus.

"Esther, Esther, come here! We have something to tell you," Ishamel called out, excitement evident in his voice.

Esther's eyes widened with anticipation as she replied, "I hope it can buy me another goat."

Ishamel and the professor exchanged glances and burst into laughter, unable to contain their amusement. They continued laughing as they made their way downstairs. Esther watched them with a puzzled expression and jokingly added, "I hope there's still wine left in the stable." This only fueled the laughter of Ishamel and the professor.

"Esther, please have a seat," Ishamel urged, trying to compose himself. He motioned for the professor to proceed.

Clearing his throat, the professor began, "Well, Esther, your family has discovered the eighth wonder of the world. And if it is proven to be authentic, your family will become very wealthy."

Esther responded with a skeptical, "Hm?"

Unable to contain the news any longer, the professor revealed, "We found a thousand-year-old drawing of Jesus."

Esther looked at both of them in astonishment, her surprise almost causing her to faint. Ishamel hurried to her side, offering comfort and a glass of wine.

The professor addressed Esther, saying, "Your husband and son can finally relax."

Ishamel added, "Abram and Jacob are in the other room discussing school, and if it's true what the professor said, then we're rich!"

The room filled with joyful cheers as they celebrated this extraordinary find.

CHAPTER 3

Jerusalem

The next morning arrived swiftly, and the professor gathered his belongings, assuring the family that everything would be fine. "Let us say a prayer, Ishamel," he suggested. The entire family stood at the door, bidding farewell as the professor prepared to leave. Ishamel turned to Jacob and warmly invited him to stay with them and work alongside them. Jacob's eyes welled up with tears at the kind offer. Abram chimed in, "Yeah, stay with us! I could use another donkey to help me around. Ha ha!" Jacob followed Abram, and Ishamel shared a laugh with Esther, remarking how they were like brothers.

Professor Eleazar arrived at his home in Al-Jib and began packing his clothes for the journey to Jerusalem. He made the necessary travel arrangements, opting to take the bus and carrying one of the scrolls. The donkey ride would have been lengthy.

During the bus ride to Jerusalem, the professor pondered over everything that had transpired and the precious item he held in his hands—a personal account of Jesus's visit to the village, with an unknown writer and artist having depicted his face and chronicled the events. He envisioned presenting the scrolls to the museum's curators, hoping they would believe in their authenticity and validate that they were not counterfeit.

Arriving in Jerusalem and making his way straight to the museum, Eleazar's hands trembled with excitement as he anticipated sharing this groundbreaking information with the scholars and curators. He was eager to let the world see the faces of Jesus, the only known drawing of Jesus and what he truly looked like.

Upon entering the main office, a short and stocky man approached Eleazar with a welcoming smile and extended hand. "Welcome, my name is Aleman, head curator of the museum, and I am very interested in what you mentioned in your cable about the discovery of the scrolls and other items. I verified your name from your village and the school where you teach. Please, come and have a seat and relax. Well, Professor Eleazar, tell me about what you have found. You sounded so excited over the phone when you arrived," Aleman inquired.

Eleazar pulled out the package from his bag and laid it out on the front table, preparing to unroll the scroll. As he began the process, Professor Aleman's eyes widened with a small smile. "Ah, a scroll from the Dead Sea," he remarked.

Eleazar smiled back and let out a little laugh. "Yes, indeed. It was found by a farmer and his son while they were grazing their goats and sheep. They noticed a hole in the cliffside of the hills that led to a cave."

As Eleazar carefully unrolled the scroll from its cloth covering, Professor Aleman observed its ancient appearance and noticed the presence of writing on it. Curiosity piqued, he wondered about the time period and year to which the scroll belonged. Additionally, he recognized that the writing was in an ancient form of Hebrew. With each revealed letter, Professor Aleman's smile grew wider. "You know, this writing hasn't been used in centuries," he remarked. "From what I can read, it appears to be telling a story of Jesus and his apostles' visit to this very village, the House of Joseph, where he was welcome to stay for dinner, in which he broke bread and drank wine with his guest and the apostles. He taught them the teachings of his Father. The guests asked Jesus questions about the laws of God and how they could strengthen their faith." As the professor continued reading, his eyes widened, and he looked at Eleazar. "Do you know what you have here?" he asked.

Eleazar replied, "Yes, please tell me more about what happened."

The text revealed that this unknown guest was also a carpenter like Jesus, but he primarily painted walls and the exteriors of houses. Eleazar asked Professor Aleman if he knew where this village was located.

Aleman responded, "Right here in Israel." Professor Aleman suggested verifying the age of the scrolls and having other scholars examine the writing to confirm their authenticity.

"Well, Professor Aleman, we have more scrolls. There are three jars full of them," Eleazar revealed.

Aleman turned to him in surprise, asking, "You have more scrolls?"

Eleazar explained, "Yes, we found three jars full, but we had to find someone we could trust. If news were to get out, you know what would happen to this family, their village, and the media attention. So if we can strike a deal for the family, you will be amazed by what the other scrolls contain."

"When can you bring the rest of the scrolls down here?" Professor Aleman asked.

"After we reach an agreement, and it has to be in writing," Eleazar responded.

Aleman then inquired about an estimate of the price the scrolls could fetch and their potential value to the farmer's family once verified. Eleazar emphasized the need to settle on a price and have it documented before releasing any more scrolls. Aleman assured him, "No, no, I understand. Believe me, I cannot price anything until we examine this scroll and any others you have."

"Professor Aleman, what I'm about to tell you is why I know you'll want to see the rest of the scrolls, and it may be hard to believe," Eleazar began.

Aleman eagerly asked, "What is it? What is it?"

Eleazar insisted on a written agreement to ensure confidentiality until a price and contract were established. Aleman agreed to have a contract prepared for the family.

"In one of the scrolls, there is a clear drawing of a man's face, and the accompanying writing identifies this person as *Yahweh*—Jesus. It is the only drawing depicting what Jesus truly looked like. It was painted by an unknown artist from the village, and we need to verify the artist's identity and the location of the village during the time of Jesus's visit," Eleazar revealed.

"Professor Eleazar, do you realize what you have? It is priceless if it's authentic and verified, not a fake. Oh my God, the only picture of Jesus. And if what you're telling me is written in the other scrolls… Oh my God, can you imagine the impact it will have? Even nonbelievers will come forward," Aleman exclaimed.

Eleazar explained that it would take weeks to verify all the scrolls as they would be sent to labs in Jerusalem. He acknowledged that some scholars might deny their authenticity, but the main concern would be the press, as news of this discovery would inevitably spread. Eleazar and Aleman agreed to share the good news with Ishamel without delay.

"Okay, when can we have the rest of the jars and the scrolls here? Don't worry, the museum will ensure security and provide a contract to work with you and the family, while keeping it as quiet as possible," Professor Aleman assured Eleazar. "Oh, Eleazar, this is going to be the eighth wonder of the world. After thousands of years with no proof of what he really looked like, the religious world will be turned upside down, and people of faith will want to see it too."

*****

Meanwhile, Ishamel anxiously awaited news at home, wondering when Professor Eleazar would inform them of Jerusalem's response. Thoughts swirled in his head, and he sought solace in the peace and quiet of the pasture near the hills. "Oh, Lord, did I do the right thing? And I thank you for leading us to this discovery as it will help my family and our village."

Professor Aleman sent the first scroll to the labs in Jerusalem for verification. The process would take approximately three weeks to confirm its age, origin, and region. Both professors eagerly anticipated the results, passing the time by discussing ancient discoveries. The weeks seemed to drag on until a letter finally arrived from the lab.

Professor Aleman eagerly opened the letter and was overjoyed to learn that the scroll was indeed authentic, dating back around a thousand years to the time of Jesus's visit to the village. The parchment was also confirmed to originate from that region. Excitedly, Professor Aleman couldn't wait to call Eleazar and share the news.

The phone rang at Professor Eleazar's home, and it was Professor Aleman on the other end.

"Eleazar, it came back! It's real and from the time when Jesus visited the village. When can you bring the rest of the scrolls? I have an agreement contract with the director of the Museum of Jerusalem, and you will be pleased with the terms for the family. I will come down to talk to the entire family about the agreement and bring the contract with me."

"So we can bring the other scroll for verification and save the last drawing as a surprise for the director of the museum. They can then make plans for a meeting of all the scholars and media, not just local but worldwide. I'll see you soon."

Professor Eleazar assured Ishamel before heading down to the village to deliver the good news to the family. He presented them with the agreement contract from the director of the museum and that he couldn't wait to obtain the remaining jars and scrolls. Only Professor Aleman knew about the drawing, and he emphasized its potential priceless value, indicating that it would bring great fortune to the family.

Esther pondered, "Hmm, will it still buy me a goat and some nice pans?"

Ishamel contemplated how the newfound wealth would change their lives. He envisioned sending Abram and Jacob to college and improving their farming endeavors with new land and equipment. However, his heart remained that of a farmer. He also had plans to assist the village by providing water and electricity to each house, as well as establishing a center for the village children and a small medical hospital. Overwhelmed with gratitude, he thanked the Lord.

"Well, Ishamel, with this money, you will be able to build and help your village," Professor Eleazar exclaimed with laughter. "Now you can fulfill your dreams and those of your children. Let's sign the contract and give praise to God, for it was His will for us to discover the cave and the scrolls."

"And, Professor, don't forget that without your and Jacob's help, we would not have this fortune. Enjoy your newfound wealth as well. Now let's make the world aware of what Jesus truly looked like."

Eleazar and the family danced and rejoiced, knowing that their dreams would soon be realized when the world sees the contents of the scroll. They anticipated the joy that others would experience as well.

Professor Aleman received word from Professor Eleazar that the family had agreed to the contract, and soon the jars and scrolls would be brought for verification. Eleazar had a surprise in store for the professor, but he hadn't revealed the details of the drawing yet.

Eleazar called Aleman to inform him that they would return to Jerusalem the following day. Before leaving, Eleazar assured the family that history would be rewritten, and he promised to stay in contact with them daily to update them on the progress.

Upon Eleazar's arrival at the museum with the jars, Professor Aleman's face lit up with excitement. He eagerly invited Eleazar inside, asking about the number of scrolls. Eleazar explained that there were approximately ten scrolls in total, but he had a surprise for Aleman regarding one of them. He hinted at the significance of the scroll and mentioned that it would require a new contract or agreement.

Professor Aleman exclaimed, "Oh my God! If this is true and verified, it's priceless!" He then questioned why Eleazar hadn't informed him earlier about this particular scroll, if he had seen it himself, and why the news had been kept secret until now.

Eleazar apologized, explaining that the scroll held immense importance to the family and the world's perception of Jesus's appearance. He emphasized the potential impact on both the religious community and nonbelievers, which necessitated careful consideration of the timing and reactions that would follow.

"So you see, it was important to keep this last scroll hidden until all the other scrolls had been verified. We wanted to ensure that the face of Jesus drawing would have the maximum impact. Professor Aleman, it's difficult to put a price on this drawing of Yahweh, and the family was reluctant to part with the scroll. I explained to them that the world needed to know, and we must share this drawing. You will need to speak to the board of directors to ensure fair compensation for the family."

"Alright, I will discuss this with them, but I won't reveal the details of the drawing until we have verified the other scrolls. Once we have completed the verification process, we will release the news to the world. Please be prepared for potential backlash as the Vatican in Rome will likely scrutinize the verification of the drawing. We need to be ready for any challenges that may arise.

"The official showing of the scrolls and the drawing will take place here in Jerusalem. Professor Eleazar, you should return to the village and make the necessary arrangements with the family. I will provide a deposit as a guarantee and ensure that they do not disclose anything to anyone prematurely. Once this information gets out, the family and the village will attract the spotlight, with reporters and the news media wanting to interview them and discover the location of the cave where the scrolls were found. We must exercise caution and be careful about what we disclose."

*****

Professor Eleazar arrived to a warm welcome from the family and shared everything that had been happening. When he showed them the deposit check, Ishamel, Abram, Jacob, and Esther rejoiced and embraced the professor. They agreed that the money should be deposited into a bank account, recognizing the positive impact it would have on the family and the village.

"Praise God for this; it will help the family and the village," Esther remarked.

They invited Eleazar to join them for a cup of warm coffee and freshly baked bread made by Esther. As they sat and talked, a peculiar glow emanated from the stable where the scrolls were hidden, and the goats and sheep began howling in joy.

Ishamel expressed his concern about the commotion, hoping the donkey wasn't causing trouble with the sheep and goats again. He instructed Abram and Jacob to investigate, feed the animals, and ensure they were given water for the night.

"Professor Eleazar, I understand why we came to you first. Alright, I will present an offer to the board of directors once the verifications are complete. Do you realize that this discovery could become the ninth wonder of the world?

"A time of repentance will come once the drawing is shown worldwide. A sense of peace will envelop both men, and now it's time to set everything in motion. I know the world will either rejoice or be shocked by this discovery. Come, Professor Eleazar, it's time to get to work. We should anticipate that other religious groups will denounce or not accept it. Also, be prepared for the influx of people coming to see you and the village where the drawing was found.

"Thank you, Eleazar, for bringing this to us first. The museum will become a highlight of the world, especially here in Israel, where Jesus was born and died for the world," said Professor Aleman. "The scrolls will be placed under high security once we turn them over to the lab. Only certain individuals and scholars will be able to view them to verify their age. There is so much research to be done, including locating the village where the artist lived and determining the time when he drew the face of Jesus.

"Numerous questions and answers will consume weeks of discussion, and the board of directors will announce a date for the press release. We will try to keep your home and family away from the media, although you know that information tends to spread. Reporters and news crews will come to the village, attempting to conduct interviews with the residents, and they will likely approach you to inquire about the location of the cave and the scrolls.

It's best that no one knows the specific area or the exact location of the cave, as the landowner might demand a substantial fee for discoveries made on their property," advised Professor Aleman. "Around here, some land is leased to other farmers who receive a small allowance for that plot. The landowner becomes wealthy, so we cannot trust them."

"You're right, Professor Eleazar. We will keep the location a secret, and I trust that our family members will remain silent. I have also spoken to the villagers about our plans for the village and the future of their children. When the announcement is made, the world will finally know what Jesus truly looked like, and crowds will flock to see," responded Ishamel.

CHAPTER 4

The Meeting

After the verification came back from the lab, confirming the authenticity of the jars and scrolls from the time of Jesus, Professor Eleazar contacted the family and shared the good news. It was now time to release the findings.

Professor Aleman gathered all the scholars in Jerusalem to corroborate the news and arranged a meeting with various religious groups, major media outlets, including the local news station, and even the Vatican in Rome. However, he was cautious not to disclose the findings until everyone was gathered in one place.

The Vatican planned to send a committee of scholars to investigate the findings and report to the Pope. Professor Aleman understood that skeptics would likely dismiss and reject the discovery. Thus, it was crucial for all the research conducted by the labs and scholars to be thoroughly examined and validated by the Vatican scholars before any conclusions were drawn.

To ensure transparency, Professor Aleman reached out to the director of the Jerusalem Museum to arrange a teleconference meeting with religious leaders from around the world. The Vatican attempted to delay the meeting until their inspectors could confirm the authenticity of all the items found in the cave.

However, Professor Aleman firmly stated that the public had the right to know. This was a significant discovery of the century, and the world deserved to be informed that a drawing, the only known depiction of Jesus, had been hidden in a cave for thousands of years. No entity, including the Vatican, had the right to keep it hidden from the public.

Everything that needed to be done has been proven to be true, and all the facts have been agreed upon by labs and scholars. Despite this, the professor remained steadfast in his decision to hold the presentation, even in the face of the threat of losing his position at the museum due to pressure from someone who threatened to cut funding by the government and other agencies.

In the weeks leading up to the meeting, Professor Aleman was bombarded with requests for interviews from the media and other officials. However, the professor remained resolute in his stance, firmly believing that only God could deliver him from these challenges. There was much work to be done, gathering all the facts and ensuring the Ishamel family was invited to the presentation. The professor said a little prayer, seeking faith and hope from the Lord.

Back in Ishamel village, word began to leak out about the discovery, and local news reporters started questioning the villagers about the details. They were eager to learn who, what, and when. Ishamel instructed his family to say nothing if anyone asked, emphasizing that it was not yet time to release any information until the presentation in Jerusalem and Professor Eleazar gave the green light. The village leaders were stunned by the sudden interest and were unaware of the details. Nonetheless, the increased attention benefited the local merchants, as many people started visiting the village.

It was challenging for the Ishamel family to keep everything a secret and unable to share with anyone. They were well aware of the potential consequences, including theft, lies, and threats. Nevertheless, Ishamel and his family were prepared to handle any situation that might arise. They took pride in the fact that their village would be mentioned and believed that, in the long run, it would benefit the community and its children. After all, they were farmers who relied on the land for their livelihoods.

"Come, come," Ishamel called his family. "Let's pray and hope for the best for all of us. Jacob and the professor are part of this family. O Lord, guide us in this quest and give us the strength to hold on together but, most of all, to help others in our fortune and create a bright future for our sons, and also Esther, the goat, and the pots and pans." Everyone laughed and hugged one other.

CHAPTER 5

Presentation Night

Professor Aleman's big day arrived, and it was a momentous occasion for Christians worldwide. The world exposition showcased the scrolls, and major media outlets from around the globe were invited with special invitations to attend. Additionally, the head of the Israeli government was informed about the event.

Despite the doubts surrounding the discovery, and the Vatican's lingering skepticism even after all the testing had been completed, the presentation went ahead in full swing at the grand hall of the museum. The parchments were carefully placed in sealed glass frames and secured with the highest level of security. The jars and other scrolls were also displayed for the public and media, reaching a nationwide audience and gaining access to international television coverage.

Ishamel and his family were prepared and proud to have their village mentioned, as they introduced the world to the painting of Jesus. However, the Vatican's acceptance of the findings, which confirmed the authenticity of the drawing of Jesus and the other relics, remained a significant milestone.

Presentation Night

Professor Aleman was filled with excitement as the media arrangements were completed, and all the invited guests took their seats. Dignitaries from various countries were present, eager to determine whether it was a forgery or a legitimate discovery. The professor anxiously awaited the arrival of the dignitaries from Rome. Ishamel and his family arrived and were seated in the front row, ready to witness the unveiling of the truth—the face of Jesus as it was seen thousands of years ago, during his time with his followers, even in his forgiving those who tormented him.

The display lights illuminated the stage as the head of the museum stepped forward to deliver the opening remarks. He welcomed the esteemed dignitaries from around the world and introduced the other scrolls that had been found. Projecting the words on a large screen, he expressed the joy of the discovery and the anticipation of seeing the face of Jesus for the first time. As the words sank in, some faces lit up, and sounds of joy filled the room.

Finally, the moment arrived to unveil the painting. A bright light illuminated a large glass frame that held the image of Jesus. As the light grew brighter, the painting became visible to the world for the first time. Tears welled up in the eyes of many in the audience while others rejoiced and praised the name of Jesus, using his Hebrew name *Yahweh*. The Almighty God was praised.

Many dignitaries and visitors looked on with both dismay and joy as they beheld the face of Jesus for the first time in the ancient scrolls, lost to Christians and the world for centuries. The Vatican delegation studied the likeness with a sense of wonder and delight.

Ishamel and his family, filled with tears, felt a deep sense of pride in discovering the painting by the will of God and now sharing it with the world. Professor Aleman, prepared for the barrage of questions, faced a flurry of cameras and flashes throughout the grand hall.

Initially, the Vatican wanted the presentation to take place in Rome while others argued for its stay in Jerusalem, the birthplace of Jesus, under the control of the Israeli government and housed in the museum. The museum director wisely formed a committee of board advisors to address all requests. Delegations from around the world expressed their desire to host the painting on tour and exhibit it to the public.

Professor Aleman patiently answered questions from the media and guests, bringing joy to Professor Eleazar as numerous countries expressed their interest in showcasing the painting. However, the Vatican remained insistent that it should be displayed in Rome as the capital of Christianity and Catholicism. Nevertheless, Israel stood firm, asserting that the painting belonged in the land where it was discovered.

The artist who created the drawing and the village from which it originated thousands of years ago received due credit. Jesus had visited this village to spread the word of God, and it was in the home of a skilled painter that his face was captured on canvas during a shared meal.

After the presentations concluded, Ishamel and his family wished to bid farewell to the professor and his staff, expressing gratitude for the memorable time in the city, the splendid hotel, and the wonders of Jerusalem. However, it was time to return home. Jerusalem is a magnificent and expansive city.

"We have animals to care for and a new home to build for our family," Ishamel remarked. "Our sons are ready for college. It's time to contribute to the rebuilding of our village and community—constructing a new school and health center for the people while preserving the old for leisurely enjoyment in their later years. We are still farmers and long to return to the lush hills where our goats and sheep graze, to breathe in the fresh morning air, and savor a steaming cup of tea lovingly prepared by Esther."

"But, Ishamel, you are wealthy," someone remarked. "You could hire people from the village to tend to your animals and manage your land."

Without hesitation, Ishamel replied, "What good is wealth if we abandon the teachings passed down by our parents and ancestors? The happiness of my family and children holds greater importance than mere money. While wealth is certainly beneficial, it can also be used in other ways to support our family and the villagers."

However, this time Ishamel and his family didn't have to walk all those miles back to the village with the donkey. They had purchased a truck in the city, and off they went, a proud family who had discovered what was deemed the eighth wonder of the world. Their mission was to bring peace and joy to the world. As Ishamel drove his new truck home, he marveled at the sight of their village and their humble abode as the sun emerged over the hills where the cave and scrolls were found, casting a ray of sunlight upon them. "Ah, we're home again, breathing in the fresh air," he exclaimed.

Upon reaching the entrance to the village, Ishamel noticed a large gathering of people lining the road leading to the village square. The entire family looked on with surprise, wondering what was happening and why the villagers had gathered. Then they heard music emanating from the square. "Oh my God, is the whole village out there?" Abram expressed concern. "I hope they're not angry with us for bringing all this to them. They might stone or hang us."

As they drew closer to the square, Ishamel saw that the village leaders were dressed in their finest attire, and the women and children were adorned with flowers. Ishamel chuckled and said, "At least they're bringing flowers for our graves."

Esther replied, "Oh, you always have to say that."

Ishamel replied, "No, no, look who's there—it's Professor Eleazar, waving at us."

When the truck stopped in the square, the crowd rushed forward to greet them. "Ah, Professor, it's good to see you again," Ishamel greeted him. "What's going on? It looks like a celebration."

The professor replied, "Yes, Ishamel, it's a celebration for you and your family, for bringing happiness and fortune to the village."

The leader of the village approached them and expressed gratitude, offering flowers and a ribbon that declared them as leaders of the village. Ishamel humbly declined, saying, "No, no, I'm just a farmer like all of you. All I want is to go back to my pasture with my goats and sheep and breathe the fresh air. We are all in this together, and we will sit down and plan new projects for the village. God has blessed us with this fortune to share with our village and friends."

With that, Ishamel suggested they enjoy the day with a prayer and indulge in some of the good village wine he spotted. The entire crowd laughed and moved to the main square, where a band was playing.

Esther held Ishamel's arm, smiling, and said, "God bless you for all of this."

As the village settled down and the sun began to set, Ishamel gazed at the hills, where the sun's rays illuminated the pasture. "Come, family, it's time to go home and settle down. It's another day, and we must care for our animals."

The professor spent a couple of days with the family, joining them in the hills and pastures, sitting, talking, and enjoying the sweet tea. Ishamel suggested, "You have a home here anytime you want to come down."

He also asked for the professor's help in planning new projects, such as a school, a community center, and other initiatives. "Come build a second home here and escape the city. This is the life to enjoy before our years slip away."

The professor expressed enthusiasm, saying, "Ah, yes, that sounds great. But I still have to assist the museum and its committee in setting up tour days for the scrolls. There is so much work to be done."

Ishamel responded, "Enough said. Let's savor the warm bread that Esther has baked for us and enjoy a special treat of hot coffee."

Abram and Jacob were already looking at colleges in the city while Esther was busy planning the arrangements for their new house on the recently purchased land. As for Ishamel, he had his new goats and pots and pans to tend to. Esther looked at Ishamel and smiled, noting that nothing had changed—he was still up early, taking the goats and sheep up to the pasture; and as always, his new truck passed by and pat the fender.

Everything was in motion for the family, and Professor Eleazar would come down whenever he had free time from the museum. He was even considering building his second home in the village. A sense of calm settled over the valley and the pasture, where the wind gently rustled the grass and the sun's rays shone upon them.

The work of the Israel museum director had only just begun. Many countries were eager to have the scrolls and display the drawing of Jesus to their people. The significance of this find resonated with millions of Christians, Catholics, and people of other faiths. It was truly the most important discovery and the eighth wonder of the world.

The museum has loaned out the display to churches around the world. People are willing to walk on their knees just to catch a glimpse of the face of Jesus. Thousands will attend the exhibition, shedding tears of joy and offering prayers. They long to see the true likeness of our Savior. Some will bring their sick and disabled loved ones, hoping for a miraculous healing. Others come with deep devotion to Christ, seeking solace and peace.

For many, this represents the second coming of Christ—a beacon of peace that calls forth nations to embrace unity. It urges individuals to turn their hearts and souls toward salvation and find comfort in the embrace of peace. There will be those who seek to discredit it, and others who will vehemently denounce it. Hatred may arise.

An unknown artist from that era captured the glory and compassion of a man who taught love while breaking bread with his host, offering sweet dates and wine as a symbol of hospitality. The artist's focus was on the face and eyes as he sketched the figure known as Yahweh, known to the world as Jesus of Israel, who gave his life for our sins.

Rolando Z Garcia

ABOUT THE AUTHOR

For many years, the author had nurtured a desire to write a book. During his time in the United Marine Corps, he learned invaluable lessons from the men and women he served with—lessons about life, duty, and most significantly, their unwavering commitment to their religion and faith.

Supported by his wife, who recognized his passion for reading, the author embarked on a quest to answer a question that had long haunted him: What did Jesus truly look like? This question inspired him to write a fictional story that depicted the appearance of Christ and explored the profound impact it would have on people's faith and the transmission of teachings to future generations.

The author expresses heartfelt gratitude to his family and friends who graciously provided feedback on the early draft of the book, contributing to the shaping of the image of Christ presented within its pages. He attributes the faith and sense of purpose necessary to undertake this endeavor to the grace of the Lord.

Rolando Z. Garcia
USMC (Ret)
Vietnam Veteran